BUZZING
RATTLESNAKES

by Ruth Berman

photographs by
David T. Roberts and David M. Schleser

Pull Ahead Books

⌐ Lerner Publications Company • Minneapolis

This book is available in two editions:
Library binding by Lerner Publications Company, a division of Lerner Publishing Group
Soft cover by First Avenue Editions, an imprint of Lerner Publishing Group
241 First Avenue North
Minneapolis, MN 55401 U.S.A.

Website address: www.lernerbooks.com

Curriculum Development Director: Nancy M. Campbell

Words in *italic type* are explained in a glossary on page 30.

Library of Congress Cataloging-in-Publication Data

Berman, Ruth.
    Buzzing rattlesnakes / by Ruth Berman ;
photographs by David T. Roberts and David M. Schleser.
        p.   cm. — (Pull ahead books)
    Includes index.
    Summary: An introduction to the physical characteristics,
habits, and natural environment of the rattlesnake.
    ISBN-13: 978-0-8225-3603-1 (lib. bdg. : alk. paper)
    ISBN-10: 0-8225-3603-X (lib. bdg. : alk. paper)
    ISBN-13: 978-0-8225-3609-3 (pbk. : alk. paper)
    ISBN-10: 0-8225-3609-9 (pbk. : alk. paper)
    1. Rattlesnakes—Juvenile literature.
[1. Rattlesnakes. 2. Poisonous snakes. 3. Snakes.]
I. Roberts, David T., ill. II. Schleser, David M., ill.
III. Title. IV. Series.
QL666.069B47 1998
597.96—dc21   97–46564

Manufactured in the United States of America
5 6 7 8 9 10 – JR – 11 10 09 08 07 06

BUZZ-Z-Z!

What is making that sound?

This is the *rattle* on a
rattlesnake's tail.

The rattle buzzes when the snake
shakes its tail.

Why do you think rattlesnakes buzz?

Sometimes rattlesnakes are
hard to see.

They buzz to tell other animals
to go away.

Rattlesnakes are *reptiles*.
Most reptiles have *scales*.

Scales grow out of the skin.

Scales are hard,
like your fingernails.

As a snake grows, its skin gets tight.
The snake must *shed* its skin.

First its eyes become foggy.
The eyes look blue.

Then the snake rubs its head
on hard places.

The skin rips, and the snake
wiggles out.

Each time a rattlesnake sheds, it adds a new part to its rattle.

How many parts can you count?

A baby rattlesnake has only
the first part of its rattle.

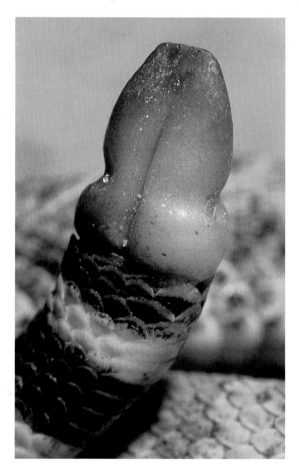

This part
is called
a *button.*

Most kinds of snakes lay eggs,

but rattlesnakes give birth
to living, squiggling babies.

Some
reptiles
crawl on
short legs.

A snake
creeps on
its belly.

When a rattlesnake hunts, it
stays still and waits.

Its tongue flicks in and out
to pick up smells.

Rattlesnakes are *pit vipers*.

You can see the pits
below this snake's eyes.

Pits feel the body heat
of other animals.

The two pits help
a rattlesnake hunt.

Watch out!
A pit viper
has *fangs*.

When it bites an animal,
poison flows through the fangs
into the animal.

The animal dies.

This rattlesnake is eating a mouse.

Snakes swallow animals whole.

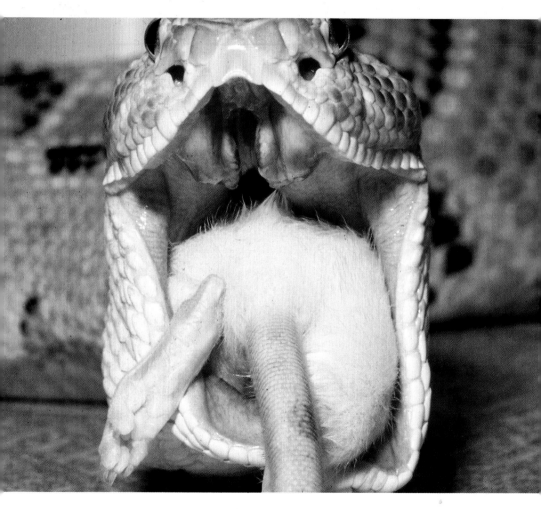

Some rattlesnakes eat only
six times a year!

Like all reptiles, rattlesnakes are *ectotherms.*

If the air is cold, their bodies become cold.

They lie in sunny spots to warm up.

Snakes do not have eyelids.
They never blink!

A snake's ears are inside its body.

The snake hears by feeling
movements in the ground.

Buzzing rattlesnakes can talk
with their tails.

They can smell with their tongues.
They can hear with their bodies.

Rattlesnakes are
amazing animals!

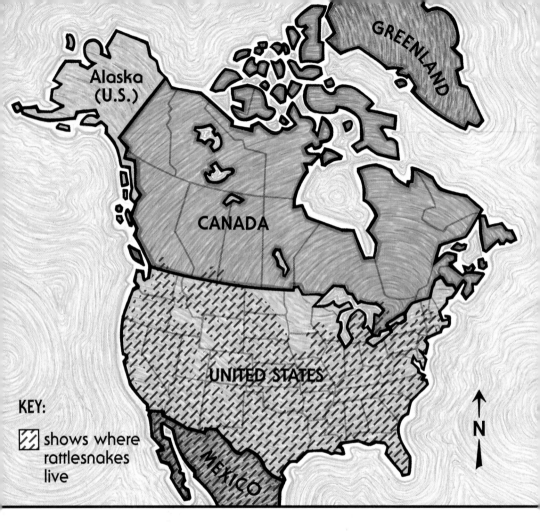

KEY:

shows where rattlesnakes live

Find your state or province on this map.
Do rattlesnakes live near you?

Parts of a Rattlesnake's Body

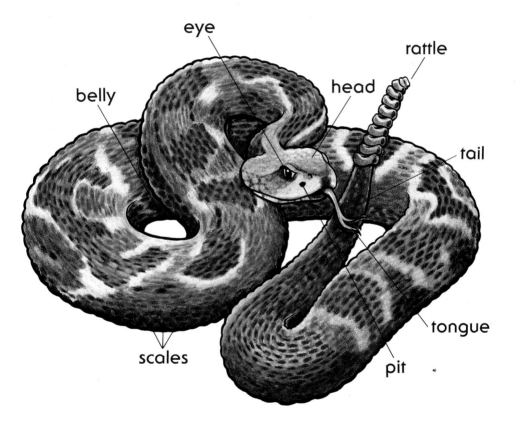

eye

rattle

belly

head

tail

scales

tongue

pit

Glossary

button: the first part of a baby rattlesnake's rattle

ectotherms: animals whose body heat changes to match the warmth or cold around them

fangs: long, sharp, hollow teeth

pit vipers: snakes that have a pit, or hole, on each side of their head to feel the body heat of other animals. Pit vipers poison when they bite.

rattle: the end parts of a rattlesnake's tail

reptiles: crawling or creeping animals that usually have scales. A reptile's body heat changes to match the warmth or cold around it. (Snakes, alligators, lizards, and turtles are reptiles.)

scales: a reptile's strong, waterproof skin covering. A rattlesnake's scales are small and flat like fingernails.

shed: get rid of

Hunt and Find

The publisher wishes to extend special thanks to our **series consultant,** Sharyn Fenwick. An elementary science-math specialist, Mrs. Fenwick was the recipient of the National Science Teachers Association 1991 Distinguished Teaching Award. In 1992, representing the state of Minnesota at the elementary level, she received the Presidential Award for Excellence in Math and Science Teaching.

About the Author

Robin Buckley

Ruth Berman was born in New York and grew up in Minnesota. As a child, she spent her time going to school and saving lost and hurt animals. Later, Ruth volunteered at three zoos and got her degree in English. She enjoys writing science books for children. She has written six books in Lerner's Pull Ahead series. Her other books include *Ants, Peacocks,* and *My Pet Dog* (Lerner Publications) and *Sharks* and *American Bison* (Carolrhoda Books). Ruth lives in California with her husband, Andy, her dog, Hannah, and her two cats, Nikki and Toby.

About the Photographers

In 1993 David and Deborah Roberts and David Schleser started Nature's Images, Inc., a natural-history writing and photography company. Their work has taken them to the rain forests and cloud forests of Costa Rica, Guatemala, and Hawaii, to the Amazon River regions of Peru and Brazil, and to the deserts of North and Central America. They research with many universities, museums, and government agencies. They also serve as expedition leaders for workshops in the Peruvian Amazon. Nature's Images is dedicated to helping people understand how fragile our world is.